The Power Of Imagination

Edited By Lottie Boreham

First published in Great Britain in 2017 by:

Coltsfoot Drive
Peterborough
PE2 9BF
Telephone: 01733 890066
Website: www.youngwriters.co.uk

FOREWORD

Welcome, Reader!

For Young Writers' latest competition, *Once Upon A Dream*, we gave school children nationwide the task of writing a poem all about dreams, and they rose to the challenge magnificently!

Pupils could write about weird and wonderful dreamlands, aspirations or hopes, or delve into nightmares. They could write about whatever they wanted, the only limits were the limits of imagination! Our aspiring poets have also developed their creative skills along the way, getting to grips with poetic techniques such as rhyme, simile and alliteration to bring their thoughts to life. The result is this entertaining collection featuring verses about everything from encounters with Robin Hood to trips to Disneyland.

Here at Young Writers our aim is to encourage creativity in children and to inspire a love of the written word, so it's great to get such an amazing response, with some absolutely fantastic poems. This made it a tough challenge to pick the winners, so well done to *Zuri Doggett* who has been chosen as the best poet in this anthology.
I'd like to congratulate all the young authors in this collection. I hope this inspires them to continue with their creative writing.

Lottie Boreham

CONTENTS

Purwell Primary School, Hitchin

Ezinna Odimgbe (8)	57
Matilda Rose Singleton (8)	58
Dylan Ramsey (8)	60
Isobella Dixon-Copping (8)	62
Oscar O'Sullivan (8)	64
Alex Wade (9)	65
Alice Vanessa Kirkbride (8)	66
Eve Barker (8)	68
Emma Marconi (8)	69
Michael Egan (8)	70
Louis Watson (8)	72
Amelia O'Fee (8)	73
Sophia Trotter (9)	74
Chenara De Silva (8)	75
Blaine Shiers-Hawkins (9)	76
Sahil Kumar Mehta (8)	77
Brooke Freedman (8)	78
Macey-Ann Cooper (9)	79
Sophie Bentley (8)	80
Cade Moore (8)	81
Morgan Waller (8)	82
Lillie Hibbard (8)	83
Caelan Murray (8)	84
Amneet Kaur (8)	85
Tilly Clancy (8)	86
Tatenda Chikaviro (9)	87

St Aidan's Catholic Primary Academy, Ilford

Daria Olatubosun (7)	88
Aarush Shounik (7)	90
Zainab Naeem (8)	91
Regina Pamba (9)	92
Saiara Sikder (9)	94
Krishna Gayatri Malladi (8)	96
Kendra Nyabowa (9)	97
Donnell James Nichols (9)	98
Emil Chaturvedi (9)	99
Chiedoziem Okoliocha (7)	100
Malaika Ann Fernandez (7)	101
Collins Olafusi (10)	102

Sylwia Blaszkowicz (10)	103
Serin Sabu (8)	104
Lilly McMorrow (7)	105
Matthew Castillano (9)	106
Haokan Zhang (9)	107
Nicola Wojtowicz (8)	108
Halle Anna Cassell (9)	109
Anirudh Sundarrajan (8)	110
Tracy Rose Brenyah (9)	111
Jonathan Anorson (8)	112
Caitlin Mottley (9)	113
Oliver Kobylinski Akintayo (9)	114
Yumna Hussain (8)	115
Ella Baptiste (8)	116
Ianna Uy Barajan (7)	117
Gabriel O'Leary (9)	118
Emaan Ali (8)	119
Tania Leo Marianesan (10)	120
Alexandra Jackman (8)	121
Britany Nkunku (7)	122
Olivia Carayol (9)	123
Tanya Chikosha (8)	124
Olivia Korzeniak (8)	125
Caiomhe Donkor (9)	126
Adam Zyrek (7)	127
Janelle Forbes (8)	128
Bismah Sohail (9)	129
Thusana Shanthakumar (9)	130
Zoé-Jane O'Leary (8)	131
Shaan Doal (9)	132
Hannah Maqsud (7)	133
Corri Ama Owusu Boateng (8)	134
Michael Jacob F Madriaga (6)	135
Remigiusz Skubiszewski (7)	136
Amara Peters (8)	137
Micah Thirugnanam Chocken (7)	138
Tisha Mohammed (10)	139
Kaci Emmanuel (10)	140
Gabriel Jai Patel (9)	141
Leah McCorkell (9)	142
'Derin Adeoye (9)	143
Eden Sofia Zerabruk (8)	144
Elton Arulseelan (9)	145

THE POEMS

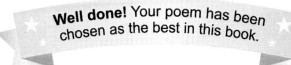

The Land Beyond The Stars

I can see a land beyond the stars
I am not dreaming
I am not dreaming
There is a land beyond the stars

Slowly shut your eyes
Really tight
Take my hand
Fly into the night

The sparkly stars
Like delicate lace
Guide you to
A chequered palace

Mumbling mushrooms
Talking trees
Are upside down
With hanging leaves

You're finally here
In front of a moon
Watch the flowers
Carefully bloom

There are weird creatures
Everywhere
Some sparkle
Some are rare

There is no bright sun
Only snow
There is noise
As the cockerels crow

I can see a land beyond the stars
I am not dreaming
I am not dreaming
There is a land beyond the stars
There is a land beyond the stars.

Zuri Bel Doggett (8)
Purwell Primary School, Hitchin

2

Fifteen Racers

I see a new, gold car, the Bugatti
I find a job and become a racer in Italy
At first I have six million Euros, so I buy the Bugatti

I was invited to the finals in Italy
I was so nervous I felt like a dead bee
I called my friend, the mechanic (Jimmy)
He's the famous mechanic Jimmy
He fixes my car and had trust in me
He mentioned to me, 'You can do this.'

I entered the race
At first I was in last place
I was zooming around again and again
Until suddenly, there was a car crash of ten cars
The next second I had a phone call
I answered it
I turned off my phone
And then I felt alone until
I was surrounded by five cars

I turned my switch onto sport mode
I was zooming but mostly daydreaming
In the next split second I woke up in bed.

Uwais Panjwani (10)

Al-Islamia Institute For Education, Leicester

A Magical Night, The Northern Lights

I walk outside one night
My dress shines like the moonlight
A beautiful butterfly lands on my shoulder
The hoots of the owls make it seem even colder
I walk and walk until I reach a field of flowers
I gasp in amazement at Mother Nature's powers
As a little fairy comes out of each one
But, it's not over yet, it's still undone
As I carry on I see a plain field
But still the magic is sealed
Though I'm feeling a whisper in the air
Saying, 'Go to the forest and see what's there!'
I walk and walk until I'm lost
Until suddenly through the frost
I see a beautiful light
Like thousands of ballerinas
Ever so beautiful, ever so bright.

Khadija Samani (9)
Al-Islamia Institute For Education, Leicester

4

Superb SATs

I don't remember how happy I was
I remember though, I was as proud as a panda
As cheerful as cheerful could be

When my teachers announced that I passed
I can't even think of a word to describe how I felt

The classroom was full of happiness and cheering
The walls made of proudness and balloons making
pops as we laughed

I felt I had made a superb, sparkling SATs achievement
Celebrating with friends
The sun is a blazing, hot ball to heat the marshmallows
The scrumptious, cranky cake filling us before we even
ate

In Victoria Park, happiness shining in the air
Smiles on all the class
As we played on the grass.

Sumayyah Chothia (10)
Al-Islamia Institute For Education, Leicester

My Best Trip Ever To The Moon!

I am waking up
The very special day is about to begin
I am going to the moon
I call my friends, my cousin and wake up my brothers
We all get ready
I pack the picnic
I call the unicorn
We all sit on the unicorn's back
It is such a fun ride
The unicorn's back is as soft as a pillow
When we get to the moon
I make a house with an ice cream roof
Chocolate bricks
And a candyfloss door
I discover the moon
I find a park and inside I find...
A rainbow slide
A chocolate swing
And a candyfloss roller coaster
We all go to the park
After the park we all have a lovely picnic
It was the best trip ever!

Hafsa Salim Chasawala (9)
Al-Islamia Institute For Education, Leicester

One Dreadful Night

One dreadful night
I was sleeping
All of a sudden
I heard some noises
Like, *huhuhuhu*
I woke up and looked out the window

When I looked out the dangerous window
I saw some drunk people sitting
I shouted at them
'Get away from here!'
They still never went
I shouted again
The same thing
'Get away from here!'

They wore bright clothes like the sun
But had ripped clothes
They had spare clothes in their bag
They even had wine in their bags

I felt scared when I first saw them
I was going to cry
But took it like a man.

Uzayr Girach (10)
Al-Islamia Institute For Education, Leicester

The Ultimate Traveller That Helps The Poor

I was bored, looking for a job
I decided to be a traveller and go around the world
I told my friend, 'Let's go travelling!'

We went to America and met Obama
We went to India and fed the poor
Next was China, I met the president
Then we went to Somalia and bought clothes for the orphans
I went to Malaysia and built houses for the poor
Finally, I went to Bangladesh, saw the poor people
Panicking for food, I felt emotional
I gave them food, money and a better outlook on life
Wow, I had the best time of my life
Now, I feel flabbergasted and elated!

Fatima Mohamed Saleh (10)
Al-Islamia Institute For Education, Leicester

A Magical Experience

I walk across the sparkling path
Flowers bloom and fairies take a bath
As I take a moment to breathe this in
The stars shine on my golden skin
I run across the fields into the woods
Until I find some special goods
In the wind my dress twirls
And my light brown hair swirls
I sprint and then jump across the lake
And so a beautiful daisy chain I make
The shiny water caught my eye
The swans swim and so I sigh
A squirrel ran up the tree
It takes a moment for you to see
As I jump into the forest
None of the rest will see the best!

Leyla Karim (9)
Al-Islamia Institute For Education, Leicester

The Trip To France!

I am going to France with my mom, dad and brother
In the aeroplane at France airport
The aeroplane was as cold as snow
I reached France and I saw the Eiffel Tower
The tower was colourful and beautiful
There was hail which felt like nails
When the hail finished we went to Disneyland
In Disneyland I went on all the rides
I saw all the mascots
The rides were smiling at people
I saw Anna with her nana
Elsa too, from Frozen
I had so much fun
We had a delicious lunch from my home
Disneyland was smelling like cotton candy.

Sarah Sarwar (10)
Al-Islamia Institute For Education, Leicester

New York Disaster

Driving to Heathrow airport
Plane departures
I do not know which terminal to fly from
Getting passports checked
Entering the aeroplane
It is like entering a stage with chairs staring at you
Sit on a borrowed chair
Buckle up your seatbelt
This is what you call a relaxing time
Air hostesses serving
Sitting in first class
Watching comedy
Rock, rock, the plane moves
Oh no! *Crash*
Plane in the Atlantic Ocean
Passengers heartbroken
This is what you call a crash!

Sumaya Ibar (9)
Al-Islamia Institute For Education, Leicester

Trip To Kenya!

I have been dreaming to go to Kenya
In the Emirates plane
To go and see my family
Now I am in the plane which is flying
In the sky
So high
Now I land in Kenya
Finally I meet my family
I see my mum's old house
It is so cool
Like my dad's pool
I went to the beach
I played in the sand
Also got tanned
I went in the sea
Got hurt on my knee
Now I'll go back to my house
In England
In the planes
Bye-bye Kenya
See you again.

Umayrah Rafique (9)
Al-Islamia Institute For Education, Leicester

Space

I see a black ocean that goes on forever
Full of stars and comets
Beauty hidden around
Through a large telescope
To gain success
Planets meeting the sun
The organisation of NASA
Icy, cold space
Soon future hotels in space
Floating around
The deep, black ocean
Feeling like a superhero
With fellow scientists
About to make a discovery
The sound of nothing about to be lost
To help people around the world
For success
In the vastness of space.

Aayan Shahab Sarwar (10)
Al-Islamia Institute For Education, Leicester

Saving A Life In Water

Swimming on the sunny beach
Having ice cream
Swimming a marathon
In the water
Which is a flowing power

Listening to sea shells
In the amazing land of Barbados
Hear the scream in the water
Swimming towards the scream like a marathon
swimmer

Saving a life
Like a life guard
Swimming fast
Coming to shore with a man

Feeling like a hero
Crying out with joy.

Abdullah Mohamed (10)
Al-Islamia Institute For Education, Leicester

My Dragon Is Red

My dragon is red
It is not dead
Then it goes to bed
In a very pink dress
Then goes to sleep
In a horrible, gross sleep
Shrinks like a bear
In his hair
Like he wants to care
As he won't share
Millions and millions are
Crowding just because
Of my dragon
Love to my dragon.

Suhaib Dahir (10)
Al-Islamia Institute For Education, Leicester

The Alien

The alien can't chew
The alien can't screw
The alien can't see
The alien can't eat
The alien is not sweet
The alien is slimy
In his dreams
The alien is crazy
In the bedroom
The alien flies to Mars
In his spaceship
The alien finds a friend
In his tummy.

Abdalla Ahmed (10)
Al-Islamia Institute For Education, Leicester

Haunted House

I had a dream that a ghost and a skeleton chased me
The ghost said, 'Most,' and 'toast.'
The skeleton said, 'Bellyton,' and 'jellyton,' which was silly
I saw a snake but actually it was fake
The snake said, 'Fake,' and 'cake.'

Yahya Gangat (9)
Al-Islamia Institute For Education, Leicester

A Journey With Wings

I believe I can fly
I believe I can touch the sky
I really can try
I have wings that I can buy
While I fly I eat a yummy pie
For some reason I see a kangaroo ahead,
But it says, 'Booo!'

Zayd Abdulla (8)
Al-Islamia Institute For Education, Leicester

I Went To The Zoo!

I went to the zoo
I saw a lion and a cheetah too
I chased them around the zoo
They met a kangaroo
I locked them in the loo
They had a nasty flu.

Abdur Rahmaan Chothia (8)
Al-Islamia Institute For Education, Leicester

The Truth About Spiders

I heard the whining of the door as it groaned shut,
I was alone; alone in my own dark hut,
The place was massive, but I knew where I was.
I was in my nightmare world, I walked down the hall,
The corridor was tall and multiple doors went past,
I was filled with dread as fear went into my head,
I stopped, eight hairy legs, giant jaws like pegs,
Standing right in front of me was a colossal spider!
And it roared at me, it chased me,
And I threw him a bag of crisps, he gobbled them,
And spat the wrapper out,
That was when I realised, he didn't want me,
He then started shrinking to the size of a pea,
I wasn't scared of him anymore,
Most spiders are more scared of me.
So don't be scared of those little creatures,
Don't be put off by their scary features,
Most of them don't bite.

Bill Wong (10)
East Park Primary School, Wolverhampton

Maths Is A Thing

When I go to bed I have a dream,
In my imaginary land where maths is a thing,
Everyone works hard and never gives up,
Because everyone believes maths is a thing,
A land where everyone's dreams always come true,
All because they always persist,

Now I begin to do my work,
Non-stop because I'm a star,
With everyone's support I know I'll be something,
Because I believe maths is a thing,
I use my knowledge to work out problems,
No one in real life knows how good I am,
Because this is my secret talent,
I see myself with long, black hair,
But can't see my maths knowledge,
I want to be like Albert Einstein, inventing equations,
believing in myself,
Now I've done all my work I now know who I am.

Riya Randhawa (10)
East Park Primary School, Wolverhampton

Spooky Night

As I walk down the long, bendy road,
Where my friend, Lyla's, party is,
I see magical cobwebs and witches' brooms,
I go in and want to go in the haunted house.
I walk over and step in the wooden door
Slam! - What was that?
The door had closed behind me.
I tried to get out but it was locked,
Then a gush of wind ran towards me.

It was as black as night,
I felt like someone was watching me.
I saw a dim light in the distance,
My worst fear was there,
Spiders.
I walked towards it.
Behind it was a door.
I told myself they won't hurt me,
I ran straight past it and out the door.

Elle Windsor (10)
East Park Primary School, Wolverhampton

Future Me

As I walked down the corridor, I saw my name
It was the same
I opened the door
And did a little more
I couldn't believe my eyes
I thought I was in someone else's life
The maid said it was time to get ready for the fashion show
I was nervous, not knowing what was going on
Lipstick and nails on
Make-up and hair done
Getting dressed and all the rest
Waiting for a limousine
It's time to shine!
Tick-tock, the clock was going on
I felt dizzy, what was going on?
I was in my room...
I couldn't believe the time had actually gone.

Sky Hendricks (10)
East Park Primary School, Wolverhampton

The Unicorn Village

I had a dream in a mystic world
Where unicorns and humans live in peace
Glitter fell from the sky onto the tiny village
Unicorns waved hello and greeted with joy
Cloud houses rose in the sky, the sweet-smelling air greeted us
The tiny village, oh so sweet
The rainbow houses glowed in the light, it was such a delight
I wandered through the candy streets
Smelling all the delicious treats
Cotton candy meadows smelt so sweet like another candy treat
The unicorns waved goodbye as my dream started to close
I forgot the mystic world where unicorns and humans lived in peace.

Emily Pugh (10)
East Park Primary School, Wolverhampton

Cadbury's Chocolate And Colourful Jelly Beans

I once was in my back garden, near the fields of corn.
I was very tired, so I started to yawn.
I was about to go inside,
Until I noticed to my side,
In the sky,
A load of brown clouds waiting to dive down and burst.

It was Cadbury chocolate I saw.
The clouds exploded and all the fun began.
I caught and tasted the chocolate drops.

Then the colourful clouds came.
Jelly beans.
I was bursting with excitement,
So much, I could have turned into a flame.

Sanchia Ellis (10)
East Park Primary School, Wolverhampton

Dreamland

In my dreamland, the skies are always blue
The sun is always saying, 'Well how do!'
The people are always happy, jolly and smiley
They may not look friendly
But they all have a heart
If you look up carefully, you'll see the unicorn god
Who makes you happy when you're sad and neutral
when you're bad
The green grass is as green as their ecosystem
Now if you fall asleep to the unicorn beat
You will wake up to a whole new you...

Talia Walker-Graham (10)
East Park Primary School, Wolverhampton

Stuck In A Dream

I woke up on a treetop,
Where I could see all flowers gleam and glow,
So I asked all the fairies where I could go,
All they said was, 'Well, I don't know.'
Not sure what would happen,
It started to rain.
All the glitter danced like a bobblehead doll,
As I met a fairy named Coll,
Zoom, went the fairies,
My dog went, 'Woof, woof!'
I said, 'I want to go home.'
And the fairy said, 'Tough!'

Addison Levy (10)
East Park Primary School, Wolverhampton

Where Dreams Are Born

Somewhere is a great magical place,
Where dreams are born,
Being free from the bad things,
You can be anyone, anything.

However, there is a dark side,
Will it escape today,
Or just whoosh when it flies away?
Where nightmares are born.

My dream shakes like a cold bird,
Screams quake,
It has escaped,
What to do,
It grows rather rudely,
This is the end of my dream,
But I won't awake!

Jasmine Elizabeth Sinclair (10)
East Park Primary School, Wolverhampton

World Of Candy

I had a dream,
It was totally sweet,
Marshmallow mountains,
Watched over chocolate rivers,
Sweet-smelling air,
No fruit, not even a pear,
Chocolate drops as rain,
There's just sweets, no more pain,
Pink wafer bricks to form a house,
For gingerbread people to live in and slouch,
Through the black Oreo window,
Gummy bears saying, 'C'mon let's go to Cookie Dough Road'
Saw liquorice car tyres roll.

Navin Chopra (10)
East Park Primary School, Wolverhampton

Kidnapped

K idnapped, I was petrified

I t was weird-looking, I wasn't with my mom

D aring, I screamed for my life, I was trapped in a van

N ot knowing what would happen, I panicked

A horrifying man put me in a bag and took me somewhere

P etrified, I started crying

P eople were muttering and bumping me side-to-side,

E ager to get out, I moved around

D eath was just around the corner.

Chenae Lewis (10)
East Park Primary School, Wolverhampton

Nightmare

N ot daring to breathe

I nside of a haunted house

G hosts gathering around me

H aunting screams coming from rooms with no one in

T errifying pictures seem to follow you

M urder weapons covered in blood

A xes, swords and knives

R ed on the ground (blood)

E veryone who had ever entered had died.

Nile Logan Ball (10)

East Park Primary School, Wolverhampton

The Thief Of My Dream

A thump was at the door,
I had to learn more,
My brother and I,
He had one eye.

He broke into the house,
With a pet mouse,
He took all my jewels,
With the tools,
Crooked teeth,
He was a thief,
I hid,
I was only a kid.

I woke up,
I had a dream,
It seemed to be real,
He was really mean...

Amelia Petgrave (10)
East Park Primary School, Wolverhampton

Dream

D readful
R est
E xciting
A mazing
M agical.

As my alarm beeps in the morn,
I forget my dreams for evermore,
I remember the start but never the rest,
But my dreams are always the best.

Katie Poole (10)
East Park Primary School, Wolverhampton

The Night I Met A Monster

Last night I had a monster dream
I got in my bed and went to sleep
I could see him in my head
I spotted a monster
As black as the dark midnight sky
He was as fluffy as five thousand cute, little kittens
His eyes were as red as a winter's fire
His claws were as sharp as five thousand steel swords
His growl was as loud as a car engine
He was as yellow as the bright morning sun
He was as spotty as a tiny, cute leopard
He was as fast as a fighter plane
I wonder what I will dream of tonight?

Max Perry (7)
Hollywell Primary School, Nottingham

Candy World

Last night I had a dream where I went to Candy World
The chocolate floor was as smooth and brown as a
grizzly bear
The popping candy trees were as green as freshly cut
grass
The strawberry houses were as red as hot Indian spices
The doors were as sharp as sharks' teeth
The liquorice windows were as black as a dark vampire
costume
The candyfloss walls were as pink as a chubby pig's
skin
I wonder what I will dream of tonight?

Henry Stokes (7)
Hollywell Primary School, Nottingham

The Wizard

Last night I had a dream where I met a really amazing
wizard
His hat was as pointy as a dangling, cold icicle
His cloak was as black as the night sky
His glasses were as shiny as a glimmering, gold jewel
His clothes were as fluffy as a grizzly, big bear
His skin was as pink as a juicy, sweet peach
His eyes were as green as swishy, long grass
His shoes were as stinky as a big, fat hippo
I wonder what I will dream of tonight?

Tayler Unwin (7)
Hollywell Primary School, Nottingham

Goose Fair 2016

Last night I had a dream where I went to the goose fair
The candyfloss was as pink as the prettiest pig
The giant wheel was as tall as the tallest tree
The lights were as bright and as colourful as fireworks
The roundabouts were spinning like cars' wheels going
round
The food smelled like beautiful flowers
I wonder what I will dream about tonight?

Isaac Brooks (7)
Hollywell Primary School, Nottingham

My Disneyland Dream

Last night I had a dream I went to Disneyland.

The castle was as tall as a big skyscraper.
The rides were as fast as a high-speed train.
The princesses were as pretty as white diamonds.
Mickey Mouse's ears were as big as the bright moon.
The characters were as happy as a Cheshire cat.

I wonder what I will dream of tonight?

Evie Marsden (7)
Hollywell Primary School, Nottingham

The Night I Met Santa

Last night I had a dream where I met Santa
His beard was as white as snow
His tummy was as round as a football
His red jacket was as red as a juicy tomato
His reindeer were as quick as a hungry cheetah
His shoes were as black as a bucket full of coal
His belt buckle was as shiny as the bright sun
I wonder what I will dream of tonight?

Erin Day (7)
Hollywell Primary School, Nottingham

A Dragon Dream

Last night I dreamed about a dragon
His breath was as hot as burning coal
His scales were as blue as the dark sky
His wings were as floppy as a pancake
His eyes were as red as an evil vampire's blood
His paws were as fierce as a great white shark
His teeth were as sharp as a razor-sharp knife
I wonder what I will dream about next time?

Charlie Corfield (7)
Hollywell Primary School, Nottingham

The Night I Met Robin Hood

Last night I had a dream about Robin hood
His top was as green as the beautiful, swishing grass
His hat was as cute as a nice, lovely kitten
His eyes were as blue as the bright, blue sea
His trousers were as grey as a little mouse
His shoes were as brown as a wooden leg
He was as brave as a fighting lion
I wonder what I will dream tonight?

Brandon Innes (7)
Hollywell Primary School, Nottingham

The Baby Leopard

Last night I had a dream where I met a baby leopard
Her paws were as soft as silky, soft cushions
Her coat was as brown and yellow as the sun in summer
Her tail was as long as an elephant's trunk
Her purr was as loud as a big, brave lion's roar
Her nose was as soft as a pink, shiny button
I wonder what I will dream of tonight?

Evie Mae Gillen (7)
Hollywell Primary School, Nottingham

The Night I Met A Dinosaur

Last night I had a dream where a dinosaur was chasing me
His teeth were as sharp as old, broken glass
His roar was as loud as one thousand people screaming
His tail was as long as a slithering snake
His breath was as smelly as an old dead rat
His eyes were as bright as the shiny, sparkly moon
I wonder what I will dream of tonight?

Alexander Skevington (7)
Hollywell Primary School, Nottingham

Chocolate Land

Last night I had a dream
Where I went to Chocolate Land
The walls were as smooth as silky skin
The floor was as bumpy as green hills
The tree smelled like strawberry sweets
The candy house was as bright as the most colourful rainbow
The chocolate signs were as brown as a grizzly bear
I wonder what I will dream about tonight?

Holly Erin Tumilty (7)
Hollywell Primary School, Nottingham

The Giant Kitten

Last night I had a dream where I met a giant kitten
His paws were as round as the big, white moon
His coat was as yellow as a bright sunflower
His tail was as long as a slithering snake
His purr was as loud as a lion's roar
His fur was as soft as a fluffy baby leopard
I wonder what I will dream of tonight?

Sophie Westley (7)
Hollywell Primary School, Nottingham

The Night I Met Robin Hood

Last night I had a dream where I met Robin Hood
He had a cloak as green as the shiny grass
He had eyes as blue as the sea
He had an arrow as sharp as a silver sword
He hid in the trees as tall as skyscrapers
He had a pointy hood, it was as pointy as a shark's fin
I wonder what I will dream of tonight?

Sophie Smith (7)
Hollywell Primary School, Nottingham

The Night I Met Robin Hood

Last night I had a dream where I met Robin Hood
His clothes were as green as a deep, dark forest
His head was as pointy as a dragon's tail
His hat was as sharp as a sword
His shoes were as black as the night sky
His belt buckle was as shiny as the golden sun
I wonder what I will dream of tonight?

Paige Carter-Angel (7)
Hollywell Primary School, Nottingham

The Giant Puppy

Last night I had a dream where I met a giant puppy
Her back was as soft as a million feathers
Her nose was as cute as pink buttons
Her paws were as round as the shiny white moon
Her eyes were as blue as the bright sky
Her whiskers were as wiry as screws
I wonder what I will dream of tonight?

Hannah Sharpe (7)
Hollywell Primary School, Nottingham

The Small Cat

Last night I had a dream where I met a small cat
His paws were as round as chocolate buttons
His coat was as black and dark as ten bats
His miaow was as loud as a dog's bark
His tail was as long as a rugby pitch
His eyes were as orange as the sun
I wonder what I will dream of tonight?

Daniel Broker (7)
Hollywell Primary School, Nottingham

The Giant Rabbit

Last night I had a dream where I met a giant rabbit.

His eyes were as round as an elephant's foot.
His tail was as fluffy as a lovely kitten.
His feet were as big as Big Ben.
He was as fast as the quickest lightning bolt.

I wonder what I will dream of tonight?

Jonathan Banner (7)
Hollywell Primary School, Nottingham

The Night I Met A Tiger!

Last night I had a dream where I met a big, brave tiger
His teeth were as sharp as a knife
He was as soft as a fluffy jumper
He was as fast as a jet fighter
His fur was as orange as the sun
And his black stripes as dark as the sky
I wonder what I will dream of tonight?

Riley Alderson (7)
Hollywell Primary School, Nottingham

The Tigress

Last night I had a dream where I met a tigress
She had black and orange fur as soft as fifty thousand feathers
Her eyes were as green as fresh cut grass
Her stripes were like a zebra crossing
Her claws were as shiny as dazzling coins
I wonder what I will dream of tonight?

Natalia Stevenson-John (7)
Hollywell Primary School, Nottingham

The Giant

Last night I had a dream about a giant
He was as tall as Mount Everest
He was as slow as a slug
He was as fierce as a lion
His hands were as large as two double decker buses
His voice was as loud as an erupting volcano
I wonder what I will dream about tonight?

George James Lally (7)
Hollywell Primary School, Nottingham

The Night I Met A T-Rex In My Dreams

The night I met a T-rex in my dreams
He was as big as a skyscraper
He was as fast as a speeding motorbike
His claws were like broken glass
He was as scary as a ghost
I wonder what I will dream of tonight?

Alex Terry (7)
Hollywell Primary School, Nottingham

Last Night I Had A Dream I Met Rudolph The Red-Nosed Reindeer

The night I met Rudolph
His nose was as red as a juicy, ripe tomato
His antlers were as sharp as a sword
His legs were as fast as a rocket shooting into space
I wonder what I will dream of tonight?

Callum Scott (7)
Hollywell Primary School, Nottingham

Captain America

Last night I had a dream
Where I met Captain America
His suit is as blue as the sky
His belt is as brown as a sparrow
His shield is as round as the moon
What will I dream of tonight?

Rhys Wright (8)
Hollywell Primary School, Nottingham

The Land Under The World

There's a place under the world
I go there every night
The land under the earth
It is a fabulous sight

There's a large bridge as big as
A squid, if you look very closely
Floating at the bottom you will see
A lion with a mane made out of weeds

Don't try and go into the dragon cave
It's guarded by a snake
If you disturb the rock face
Cover your eyes and ears when it wakes

The crafty trees hover over your skinny legs
To trip and tip you is their aim
Keep focussed on the burning wings
To beat them at their game
Come and join me in my land
Under the world
I go there every night.

Ezinna Odimgbe (8)
Purwell Primary School, Hitchin

Once Upon A Cat

Underneath my eyelids
Is a land of imagination
But tonight will be the best
Oh yes, the best of them all

I was in a kitchen
Near a mouse hole
Being a cat
With eyes like coal

After my wait
My mouth opened wide
I staggered to my room
Under my duvet I hide

First day of school
I walk down the street
When I get there
I sit in my seat

I stare at my class
They stare at me
'A cat in the school,' some whispered
But what cat I see?

Another cat!
She did a wink
The teacher fetched
Herself a drink

After school
We had a chat
Her name was Chenara
For we are both cats

I am tabby
But she is grey
I brought her some fish
On a tiny tray

Then I woke up
I gave a sigh
What a lovely dream
So again I shut my eyes.

Matilda Rose Singleton (8)
Purwell Primary School, Hitchin

The Land In My Dream

The land in my dream
Is a wonderful place to be
I climb aboard a pirate ship
It's a wonderful place to see
Warm sunshine and sparkling waves
It's a wonderful place to me

I discover a deserted island
I walk along a beach of black sand
With my brothers and a trained troll
We fall down a deep, dark hole

Surrounded by shadow men
With shadow magic they lure us in
To a place where the shadow men live
And a large place to trap us in

Dead trees surround us
An opening leads me to hope
Of returning to the seas
And back to my boat
The sun fades and the moon shines
A ghostly galleon across the skies

I'll get back across the sea
I'll go back to my beach

Where everything's wonderful
And that's the world you'll see
You'll see
You'll see
You'll...
See...

Dylan Ramsey (8)
Purwell Primary School, Hitchin

The Nightmare Gate

Where am I? What is this?
It's so beautiful
It feels like bliss
Lots of flowers dancing

I spot some people
Dressed in white
They have top hats
One flew a kite

Is that a grey gate?
I go through, *creak, bang!*
This world is full of hate
Oh no! This place is as black as the night sky!

I don't like this world
It's the opposite of the other side
I want to go home
I need to hide

After I hid behind a gravestone
The lightning leapt from the sky
I felt so scared, I was all alone
Is this happening or is it a dream?

I want to wake up and escape
I need to feel safe in my cosy bed
Am I good, am I evil?
Or is this all in my head?

Isobella Dixon-Copping (8)

Purwell Primary School, Hitchin

A Land In The Skies

I slowly close my eyes
I'm transported to a lonely land
A land in the skies
With flying cardboard boxes

A massive magical castle
The cardboard boxes with wings
Which look like a flying parcel
Oh no! A dragon's taking me in

I creep into the castle
And say hello to the king
Who only has one eyeball
Watching me with his ruby ring

An old oak tree flew in through the window
And grabbed me with crooked hands
My adventure is nearly up
In this amazing dream land

I will never forget this dream
I walk downstairs
And get my hot chocolate and cream
I hope I go back there.

Oscar O'Sullivan (8)
Purwell Primary School, Hitchin

The Boy That Dreamt About Roblox

A boy that went to bed
And put a pillow under his head
A gate opened with a creak
He heard a mouse, *squeak*

The boy walked up the stairs
Where he met two brown, grizzly bears
As he had no fear
Soon the bears started to disappear

The boy knocked with his fist
Like a drummer with a beat
Bang, bang, bang!
Open wide, such a sight

The boy woke up
Got up out of bed
Ran down the stairs
Skeletons everywhere

The boy said, 'Skeletons.'
They talked and talked
He wasn't scared
So they danced until the night ends.

Alex Wade (9)
Purwell Primary School, Hitchin

Imaginary World

There's a place I want to take you
I go there every night
In my imaginary world
It is an extraordinary sight

There's a large lake as black as coal
If you look in the lake
It is very magical
In my imaginary world

Don't attempt to climb Mountain Eve
It's guarded by a big fish
Surrounded by purple pools
Where you can make a wish

Imaginary people can fly
Up in the sky
Going around in a magical car
In my imaginary world

In my imaginary world
I can do anything
I can do

I can
Do

Anything...

Alice Vanessa Kirkbride (8)
Purwell Primary School, Hitchin

Once Upon A Cat's Dream

There's a place I want to take you
It's the best place I've been
So I'm going to fly you across the clouds
To the land of my dream

You can see mice as white as ice cream
Street lights are ruby red lasers
Mean bugs having bad dreams
And me chasing wind-up racers

Best of all are streets
Lined up with fluffy beds
And raindrops taste of treats
You always get fed

In my dream world
There are no dogs
Or anything to hurt you
No boys with nets
No scary vets

That's a place I want to
Take you.

Eve Barker (8)
Purwell Primary School, Hitchin

Dream Drawings

One night a girl was drawing
In her bedroom
While the world was sleeping
The midnight moonlight
Lit up her paintings
She never noticed
At first...
But soon
Her room
Had been painted brown
The chocolate drawing
Had melted and was
Dripping off the walls
The sketch of her dog
Began to bark and
The cat picture heard its calls
The gingerbread man jumped
On Emma's head
And started jogging
On the spot
He sprang higher and higher
Until on the window sill he got
Then he jumped out the
Window and into the night.

Emma Marconi (8)
Purwell Primary School, Hitchin

The Odd Place To Be

A boy asleep
Having a dream
Where swords could talk
And toys were boys

Some robots come
And kick a crumb
Then they die
While people fly

Colossal hens
And tiny men
Fighting pizza
On the freezer

One horse says
'I lost my head.'
While buildings would fight
Nearly all night

Someone flies off
Like a fast moth
Then he got found
And didn't make a sound

The boy woke up
And saw his pup
Then his dog leaped
Yawned, went back to sleep.

Michael Egan (8)
Purwell Primary School, Hitchin

The Magical Lego Land

Once I got teleported
To a magical Lego Land
Where people were made of
Plastic bricks for their dinner

Trees had square leaves
Birds ate plastic berries
People were stuck to the ground
Until giant hands picked them up
Cars had square wheels
It's a bumpy journey

All the roads are straight
To the pirate ship
The ropes were made of rubber bands
The captain was scary
There was a hole instead of an eye

Plastic sword and frozen people
About to walk the plank
I hope I get out alive...

Louis Watson (8)
Purwell Primary School, Hitchin

A New World

Shut your eyes
And drift away
Count some sheep
For on your way

Just think of the best
And here you are
A five way road
And rainbow cars

A circle house
The bestest place
For peace and quiet
In this wild case

Leaves as square as a box
Trees that float in a muddle
The wind is like a pouncing fox
And the world is like a puzzle

A sizzling sun
As flat as a pancake
Dripping rain pouring upwards
To the concrete lake
Shut your eyes
And drift away.

Amelia O'Fee (8)
Purwell Primary School, Hitchin

Candylicious

Candyfloss trees
Can actually sneeze
While chocolate dogs bark
And ride caramel sharks

You can eat sweets
That are the most fantastic treats
But give them good care
Because once there was a hare
That went everywhere
And ate everything in Candyland

The chocolate lake
Is full of cake
That you can eat and
Eat and eat

Take a trip to Candylicious
But please don't be suspicious
It's a place full of fun
And bubblegum
You can eat everything you see!

Sophia Trotter (9)
Purwell Primary School, Hitchin

The Opposite Dream World

I woke up this morning
Feeling a bit confused
I turned into a cheetah
And completely had a different colour

I had black spots like charcoal
Then a long tail started to grow
I was smooth, now I'm furry
But it's easy to get food

I had terrible teeth
When I screeched
The whole jungle heard me
But then water, water I reached

I saw my reflection in the water
My wiry whiskers started to show
My tongue as red as ruby
And my green eyes reflected back.

Chenara De Silva (8)
Purwell Primary School, Hitchin

When I Close My Eyes

As I slip into a deep sleep
The dreams start to unfold
Colours flashing by
No baby will ever cry

Animals, talking trees
And houses walking
Football games never ending
My name's the one that's trending

Flying cars and people living on Mars
All fun and games, no one ever complains
As I park my rocket on the drive
I think, wow, I'm alive

The dream fades away into a brand new day
I can't wait for bedtime again
So I can go back and play.

Blaine Shiers-Hawkins (9)
Purwell Primary School, Hitchin

Electric Invader

There is a place that I go
I go every day and night
The world is a good sight
With lots of bright lights

The lightning gives power for my world
The road is as blue as the sea
And the cars are as fast as rockets
Blasting, blasting by

There were some rusty robots blue and lime
Their heads were full of sticky slime
Their colours were divine
Shooting and scampering

There is a place that I go
I go every day and night.

Sahil Kumar Mehta (8)
Purwell Primary School, Hitchin

My Nan And Candy Land

As I shut my eyes
With Nan beside
As we lie
With my nan and we dream

Clouds take us away
For a year and a day
To a land
With chocolate and cream

Sherbet white as snow
The chocolate lake was low
Drunk with straws
And it dripped on the floor

Gummy bears
Hide in the forest
Made of candy cane trees
With jelly bean bees

Candy Land is the place to be
And full of ice cream and dreams.

Brooke Freedman (8)
Purwell Primary School, Hitchin

The Galaxy

As I fall asleep
To the galaxy I go
The galaxy I sweep
As the stars come and go

I go to a special place
Down the midnight path
Like a falling raindrop
It's in outer space

I go there every night
Strange land I roam
It's an amazing sight
It's like my home

The galaxy is beautiful
The stars shine in the moonlight
Like a night light
It's an amazing sight.

Macey-Ann Cooper (9)
Purwell Primary School, Hitchin

The Elephant's Dream

Sleeping under the stars
So bright
In the dark of night
An elephant leader and her herd
Dreamt of a peaceful world

A world where tusks grow long
And there are sweet songs
Of the baby elephants
Playing in the dust
Shading from the sun

Staring into the
Victoria Falls
Admiring their tusks
Standing proud and tall
No bangs, no booms, no guns
The elephants are free to roam.

Sophie Bentley (8)
Purwell Primary School, Hitchin

My Magical World

Shut your eyes
Really tight, ready
To make your dreams
Come true

In the magical forest
With talking trees
Telling me to jump into
Books to make my dreams
Come true

The crunching of the papers
As I dived into the book
Like a dolphin in the waves
So my dreams come true

The emerald leaves
With hooting owls
And behind the dark trees
Glowing eyes were there.

Cade Moore (8)
Purwell Primary School, Hitchin

My World

When I close my eyes
And dream
I dream
I am carried
Down
Down
Down
Away from my bed and my sleep

I arrive with a bump
On the soft, green grass
A little red door
In the middle of the floor
That I have never seen before

A tiny fairy
Stood glowing outside
She danced elegantly
Like a flickering flame
And suddenly disappeared
What a shame!

Morgan Waller (8)
Purwell Primary School, Hitchin

Drawing Dreams

In my dreams I see my pencils
Drawing on my walls
I hear them scratching like a rat
And then the wise owl calls

My eyes slowly start to open
My paintings come out, off the wall
I started to freak out
And then the wise owl calls

Tall paintings were standing
As still as statues
At the end of my bed
They needed new colours
So I grabbed my paintbrush instead.

Lillie Hibbard (8)
Purwell Primary School, Hitchin

A Dog's Dream

On the sofa
Come with me
To a magical land
Where treats hang on trees

Where cold water runs
Endless fields grow higher
Just for me to admire
Sausage grass grows
Just like a rose

Chasing old chickens
For centuries
Endless bones
Come and go

Tennis balls
Launch
For me to catch
With my friend
Matilda.

Caelan Murray (8)
Purwell Primary School, Hitchin

The Magical Dream

I came to a forest
That was enchanted
Butterflies dancing around
With wings that sparkled
Like shimmery diamonds

Trees stay still with
Tall, twisted branches
With magic glitter
Shining bright in the sky

I saw a deer jumping
It was really shy
She had chestnut eyes
Then gave a sigh.

Amneet Kaur (8)
Purwell Primary School, Hitchin

The World Without

Imagine a face without a mouth
No one could speak
Imagine a plane without wings
No one could go anywhere
Imagine a clock without hands
No one could tell the time
Imagine a tree without a trunk
No squirrels could climb it
Imagine a house without windows
The rain could come in
Imagine a world without...

Tilly Clancy (8)
Purwell Primary School, Hitchin

The Dreaming Cat

I am a cat
Curled up in the grass
Who dreams of climbing trees

Of peaceful days
With no one around
Where I can do
What I please

Of hundreds of mice
Running around
All for me to play with

I hope my dream
Will happen again.

Tatenda Chikaviro (9)
Purwell Primary School, Hitchin

Rainbow Dash And The Black Cloud Race

One day I saw Rainbow Dash, busting out of the clouds in a flash
It was the most beautiful sight
As Rainbow Dash shone in the shimmering sunlight.
I felt so comfortable and full of care
As Rainbow Dash looked at me and said, 'Hi there.'
I used my wings to soar into the sky
As I looked down and I was ever so high.
Rainbow told me it was okay
As the race bell rang Rainbow said, 'This way.'
Every Pegasus pony at the line was stretching their wings
As Rainbow said, 'I'm going to win those golden rings.'
The gun had been shot, how many clouds need to be dodged?
Don't know because there were quite a lot.
Rainbow Dash dodged the black clouds very fast, then she bumped into one
Then she fell down, and the rings, she will have none.
I flew down to save Rainbow Dash
Then we won the race in a flash.
We finally got the golden rings

As on each side there were golden wings.
I said it's time to go
Then we went happily home.

Daria Olatubosun (7)
St Aidan's Catholic Primary Academy, Ilford

Spooky Haunted House

S tuck in the mirror maze which is dying with horror
P etrified with fear
O utstanding tricks
O nce you're gone, it's for the bad
K illing vampires who suck your blood
Y ou need to run from the hungry wolf

H at tree will take your hat so beware
A ll will get burned by the hot fire
U naware of the haunted kingdom
N ever get caught by the petrifying witches
T his house is full of monsters I tell you
E veryone, you should run away
D eadly dragons roam the house

'H elp!' you'll shout, 'help!'
O ut of the house if you know the way
U nwilling to be trapped in this haunted house
S cary ghosts as white as a feather
E ating trolls which eat you to death.

Aarush Shounik (7)
St Aidan's Catholic Primary Academy, Ilford

The Red Carpet

O ne day we had to go to the red carpet
N ever ever have I gotten that crowded
C amera lights were flashing everywhere
E veryone was really loud

U pon the red carpet
P eople were screaming when Zayn Malik came, I love Zayn
O ne hour later Gigi Hadid came
N ever have I been so tired

A lthough the red carpet was really amazing

R ed is also my favourite colour
E ven though my brother was really tired
D avid Beckham came as well

C ameron Dallas came, I love him
A nd we are having a good time
R emember me, Zayn Malik
P atrick my brother was lost now
E ven I want to go home
T omorrow is in one hour!

Zainab Naeem (8)
St Aidan's Catholic Primary Academy, Ilford

Me, The Tiger

Me, the tiger, a minuscule cub
Hidden in a tiny syllabub
Running freely
My mum chasing dearly

In the distant marshes
My siblings in branches
Shrieks of joy
From all the boys

When dusk
Turned to a nightly musk
I saw a man
I ran

I saw the glint of terror
In his eyes of error
The blade
While he waded towards me

He stabbed me in the tummy
I cried for my mummy
The wails
Muffled in the bales

In a car
Going far
To a place
Maybe in space

I missed my syllabub
In the hubbub
I fell asleep
While eating meat

I'm now on display
Forever in dismay

In a place where I'll
Never belong.

Regina Pamba (9)
St Aidan's Catholic Primary Academy, Ilford

Candyland

The start of my dream
Flowers are beautiful
Giving me plentiful
Ahh, what a start!

Going with my besties
All packed up and ready
Ready to go mate?
Off we go to Candyland

Landed at Candyland
The place you eat!
Everything's edible
Oh it's all free!

Love it all
Taste it all
I played on all of the rides
Yummy though!

There's a jelly jungle!
Tree leaves that are candyfloss!
The buttercups taste like butter!
The grass is sprinkles!

Time to end it
What a day
Truly it was amazing
Maybe I'll come back,
Another day!

Saiara Sikder (9)
St Aidan's Catholic Primary Academy, Ilford

My Day At The Water Park In The Dream

My dream is in a water park
Oh good, 'cause the shoes I'm wearing are from Clarks
I am with my new friend
I hope that we will blend

Mum said, 'Have lots of fun.'
But I hope I don't melt in the sun
Dad says, 'Let's do this.'
I say that Mum I will miss

Mummy's not coming
But she is still loving
Bro is funny
Oh butterflies in my tummy

Whatever so I'll face it
And make sure I embrace it

Suddenly I drowned
Felt like I was underground
But I got up, I got a grip
And did not rip
I loved it!
Best experience ever!

Krishna Gayatri Malladi (8)
St Aidan's Catholic Primary Academy, Ilford

My Family

When I was a little baby, I began to see
That I had a special family who was always there for me
A family who was by my side and was always there
A family who was nice to me and wouldn't give me a scare

I love my family and I know they love me too
And even if I had to pick one member, I could not choose
My family means the world to me and I wouldn't know what to do
If my family had left I wouldn't know who to turn to

Everything I do is for my family only
And without them I would be very lonely
I am really lucky to have a family like mine
And I will still be lucky from time to time.

Kendra Nyabowa (9)
St Aidan's Catholic Primary Academy, Ilford

The Last Death Of Kid Army

We are at school, playing pool
The lights are on, the teachers are gone
I wanted tea
Until I saw a pea
I saw stuffing, inside a muffin
A ghost appeared and asked for some toast
So I gave him my roast
I saw a cap
The PE teacher said, 'Give me a lap'
I saw mice, eating ice
I found a chain, in the rain
It read 'Pain'
My life is full of strife
I have bones made out of stones
I saw raindrops on a leaf
It reminded me of the Coral Reef
I saw a label
In a stable
Then I had a Fanta
And drank it with Santa.

Donnell James Nichols (9)
St Aidan's Catholic Primary Academy, Ilford

The Lab

I was in a lab
With a slab
Where there was a scientist
Who pushed a button

There was a bang
There was a crash
There was a boom
There was a crack

The world turned red
Like fresh blood
Then the scientist hit it again
The world was blue

Crack! The world was green
Bang! It was orange
Crash! It was pink
Then it was white

Bang, boom, crack
I was a rainbow
Then the scientist said, 'End, end.'
And that was my alarm for school.

Emil Chaturvedi (9)
St Aidan's Catholic Primary Academy, Ilford

Empire's Great Alien

A big alien that blops, plops, pops, bops
A big alien that has ricebots, micebots, that turn him little
A big alien
A big alien that moans, groans and loans
A big brute that loots his chute
A big alien that cries into soap
A big alien that bullies
A big alien that glooms and looms
A big alien with cans and fans
A big brute that watches the knight in the night
A big alien's name is Jose Pose Hose
A big alien that speaks and sniffs
A big alien that lives in Westminster
An alien that is a silly billy
An alien that is rash and dash.

Chiedoziem Okoliocha (7)
St Aidan's Catholic Primary Academy, Ilford

Lunch With A Lion

One lovely day, I just wanted to get some grain
To bake a cake
Suddenly there was a knock on the door
Who could it be?
It couldn't be my friend Lee
I opened the door, a lion!
He said his name was Ryan
At first I screamed
And then I beamed
He said, 'Come on, let's munch some lunch.'
I said, 'Okay I've made a wonderful cake.'
He said, 'Why didn't you tell me before?'
I said, 'Okay, let's bring this outdoors.'
He said, 'Yes, let's have a picnic.'
It was so wonderful.

Malaika Ann Fernandez (7)
St Aidan's Catholic Primary Academy, Ilford

The Sandwich Monster

Eating a sandwich, what a delight
But there becomes a horrible fright
Quickly good turns to bad
The scariest day I've ever had

The sandwich comes to attack
Their horrid tongues lick my back
They want my body to devour
I have to use all my power

I ran away to cry for help
I should have just eaten kelp
I shout that there is danger here
But all they do is laugh and jeer

I guess now they have won
Now all my life is done
I'm in the stomach of a beast
Now I am a giant feast.

Collins Olafusi (10)
St Aidan's Catholic Primary Academy, Ilford

Colourful Pictures!

I can see loads of pictures of William Morris
Banging, shaking with colourful colours

I am with my family
I've got to see the pictures
How could I believe it?
This is impossible

I am inside a studio
Where it is fun
With crackling and backing
Say it will be beautiful

Come, come
It will be colourful
Don't make a mistake
Give it a try

I don't care
I am scared
There's some colourful people standing by me
Saying it's a beautiful picture.

Sylwia Blaszkowicz (10)
St Aidan's Catholic Primary Academy, Ilford

Candy Palace

I had a dream of a candy palace
I was given a tour by an elephant made of candy
I saw candy cane trees and lollipop flowers
I also saw chocolate rivers flowing down jelly
mountains
The floors are made of ginger
The houses are made of candy

I was so hungry I stopped for a break
I ate some lollipop flowers and licked some candy cane
trees
I waited for the soda volcano to erupt
Then I heard *boom!*
The volcano erupted and erupted a lot of soda
I drank a bit then I thought it's time to go.

Serin Sabu (8)
St Aidan's Catholic Primary Academy, Ilford

The Blue Man With A Fading Tan

One night I was sleeping in my bed
When suddenly I was having a meeting
There was the type of man
Who was wearing a fading tan
And he was a blue man
Then he picked up a stick
And the stick ticked
I fell into a dream
Where he was very mean
He shouted like a giant
But he seemed very quiet
He took me to a small place
It looked very black
I went into a light
There was a tiny flash of darkness
In the darkness there was a dash of light
Was this a dream?
Or was it a true thing?

Lilly McMorrow (7)
St Aidan's Catholic Primary Academy, Ilford

Dragonland

It's Dragonland, Dragonland
Who can you meet?
The angriest dragons
Just like me.

There is a mad scientist
What can you do?
All you can do is run away

The volcano, volcano
Run to it!
It's the only place
You can live.

Dragons, dragons
Listen to me
We must team up
To save your friend

Please don't take dragons
Don't take my friends
Please don't let
It happen again!

Matthew Castillano (9)
St Aidan's Catholic Primary Academy, Ilford

The Executioner

I saw the executioner
Dressed in black
Without any fright
I screamed in the night
I saw his eyes of error
And of my cries of terror
I knew I was dead
But I was in my bed
Screaming, screaming
What else can I do?
He said his evil words
No one ever heard
About him again
He was in my head
Forever again
My best mate
Lost his fate
At his rate
He said his evil words
He heard no one
Calling his name
This is no game.

Haokan Zhang (9)
St Aidan's Catholic Primary Academy, Ilford

Candy Crush

I had a dream, of ice cream,
And ginger houses with strawberry sauce.
I was riding on a candy dragon with a yellow Pikachu!
We were in The Sour Palace of the Sour Queen,
When we destroyed her we were eating the mountains
Chocolate and cookies, with delicious ice cream!
I loved that place and it was a dream!
But still it didn't end,
I'm still here!
It was amazing there,
And when I wake up I'll remember
That magical place with cheer!

Nicola Wojtowicz (8)
St Aidan's Catholic Primary Academy, Ilford

The Kidnappers Dressed In Black

T ime passed
H ell arrived
E xcitement drops

K illing kidnappers dressed in black
I n the cinema
D evils help the kidnappers
N ervous people from afar
A fter they take me
P articular thoughts come again
P reparation takes too much time
E ver going to be left again
R unning around on the street
S aw the kidnapper in my dreams.

Halle Anna Cassell (9)
St Aidan's Catholic Primary Academy, Ilford

Dragon Adventures!

D eadly adventure

R uined city

A dventure saved

G reat stealth

O utstanding performance

N eed for speed

A crazy danger

D aring rescue

V ile terror

E normous monster

N ight fury

T error of the world

U tterly dangerous

R iddle of the high seas

E xciting adventure

S tealth of the dragon.

Anirudh Sundarrajan (8)

St Aidan's Catholic Primary Academy, Ilford

The Nightmare!

T he dream I once had

H ave never seen before

E ating my dinner, fire here, fire there

N ever experienced this before

I scream for God's help

G onna get her back

H ave you ever seen this before?

'T rack her down,' I say

M ummy, I yell

A fter my death

R un away, what do I do?

E ver gonna love God again?

Tracy Rose Brenyah (9)
St Aidan's Catholic Primary Academy, Ilford

I'm Going To The Moon To Get Stuck

I'm going to the moon with my balloons
I hope I come back soon
There's only hope in June
I go to the moon, I get stuck
I need a tea cup
I want to say to my friends, 'What's up?'
I know I'm a bit whingy
But I need to be cringy
I miss my wife
I need to save my life
Oh please, oh please can you get me out of here?
I need to taste my wife's dinner
Her roast chicken is a winner.

Jonathan Anorson (8)
St Aidan's Catholic Primary Academy, Ilford

Fairyland

In Fairyland who will you meet
A beautiful fairy as lovely as me
The only place that you want to be
Fairyland, Fairyland, an amazing dream
Down in the depths of the Fairyland lake
An evil fairy lay awake
I feel a shiver
I feel a shake
The evil fairy is coming
Out of the lake
She'll take my powers
She'll take my friends
Please don't let it
Happen again!

Caitlin Mottley (9)
St Aidan's Catholic Primary Academy, Ilford

Kites And Flames

One restful night I saw a kite
And people fight

I saw a light in the night
I was right but not quite

I was low but fine
I could flow but I always said, 'Hi!'

I was flying
And people were crying
I saw a bouncy ball on the pool
And my friends had pens

I was strong
But a bit wrong
About the restful night.

Oliver Kobylinski Akintayo (9)
St Aidan's Catholic Primary Academy, Ilford

The Chocolate Universe

This is a dream
What is the theme?
I like eating chocolate sweets
More than staying home to read

I like eating chocolate food
More than eating old soup
Always eat chocolate sweets
Don't be lazy and start to weep

Always eat chocolate sweets
Never eat Shredded Wheats
I like eating chocolate food
More than staying at home for a snooze!

Yumna Hussain (8)
St Aidan's Catholic Primary Academy, Ilford

The Park...

A park full of fun
I see people
From the world above
Flying saucers all around
Captain Underpants flying out

I'm with Megan Trainor
Who is my mum
I have a sister called Charra
She's really fun

At Olympic Park
Having fun
Pop stars are at the park
Aliens taking over
Me and you at the park
With my sister and my mum.

Ella Baptiste (8)
St Aidan's Catholic Primary Academy, Ilford

Ice Cream Disaster

I ce cream
C ousins
E xciting

C ream
R oundabout made out of ice cream
E lated
A n ice cream
M onsters

D isaster
I ce
S avage monsters
A mazing
S tuck in an ice cream cage
T errible
E gg monster
R otten egg monsters.

Ianna Uy Barajan (7)
St Aidan's Catholic Primary Academy, Ilford

The Big Fright Fight

It was the last day of school and me and my mate were
late
And after school we went to see a bull
Late after school we went into the pool
I couldn't wait till Fright Night
Because it was my night at Fright Night
I got into a little fight
With Geoffrey on my right
It was the scariest fight on the scariest night
I got a big fright
I went on Stealth by myself.

Gabriel O'Leary (9)
St Aidan's Catholic Primary Academy, Ilford

I Know You Once Upon A Dream

I know you once upon a dream
I want to see you laugh not scream
Even though you do overnight
I still know you as light
I see you once upon a dream
And if you tell a lie
It will spread throughout the world
Like a zombie
Grabbing my knees and going back in time
And my best friend kicks the clock and *whoosh!*
I'm back home to my home, sweet home.

Emaan Ali (8)
St Aidan's Catholic Primary Academy, Ilford

Fairy Wonderland

Waterfalls flowing,
Leaves blowing,
Big caves,
And fairies that are brave.

Searching around,
On the ground,
Little leafy plants,
And trees that dance.

Up and down,
Searching around,
Creative colours,
Up in the clouds.

Rainbows shine,
Like a bright light,
Twinkling lights,
Will shine tonight.

Tania Leo Marianesan (10)
St Aidan's Catholic Primary Academy, Ilford

The Country Of Madness

I wake up in a land
Like no other, a magical, lovely, mad country
Where clouds and grounds are candy
Zombies roam the Earth
And tornadoes fly around the solar system
I hold my bear as tight as ever
And I just want to leave until a zombie grabs my knees
I scream and cry
And my teddy flies
He hits a clock
It make a noise
Then I'm back at home.

Alexandra Jackman (8)
St Aidan's Catholic Primary Academy, Ilford

Spy Time

I suddenly opened the door
Then I saw a claw
After I saw a magic door
Then I opened the door, I saw a bouncy ball
Then this lovely girl
Took me to her home
She had a kitty cat and it took a nap
The girl's name was Bella
Then she told me that she was a spy
She took me to her super spy palace
Then I became a spy
It was so fun to be a spy.

Britany Nkunku (7)
St Aidan's Catholic Primary Academy, Ilford

Forest Of Might

Playing in the meadow, happy and bright
But suddenly we saw a sparkling light
Then we got so excited with delight
Then we jumped in a forest with might
Where there is possibility of flight
We can fly ever so high
Across the sparkling sky
We feel so free and happy with glee
Our spirit rose like a blooming tree
Cool and light, the breeze is alright.

Olivia Carayol (9)
St Aidan's Catholic Primary Academy, Ilford

A Day Out In Candy Land

In front of my eyes there are...
Lollipop trees
And candyfloss clouds
Also lickable gobstopper grounds
Marshmallow sofas
Inside gummy brick houses
Queen Candy's sherbet castle, lovely and sweet
Glitter, my sugar unicorn, and lots more people to meet
Mr Gummy Bear and Mrs Haribo Love Heart, deeply in love
And their children Kayla and Dove.

Tanya Chikosha (8)
St Aidan's Catholic Primary Academy, Ilford

The Deep Candy Dream

Candyland, it's like Mandyland (but candy)
Jelly, it's good for my belly
I like the candy rhyme, but it's a waste of time
Toxic waste with a lovely taste
Birds love nerds
Winders are in beloved binders
I knocked on a door, I saw before
Gingerbread men, a name tag, Ben
I was sad and mad
Cotton Mandy, you mean cotton candy!

Olivia Korzeniak (8)
St Aidan's Catholic Primary Academy, Ilford

Fly

Playing in the hills
Running past the mills
Making flower crowns
Without a frown
Climbing up a tree
We feel so free
We could see the homes
See the gnomes
The branches are breaking
My heart is aching
We can fly, we can fly
Ever so high
Cool and bright
The breeze is light
In the sky
I think I might die!

Caiomhe Donkor (9)
St Aidan's Catholic Primary Academy, Ilford

Scared At Night

One restful night
In the light
I saw bright red blood
I did not know what to do
I am scared
I am trapped in this place
I am the best
I am the worst
I don't want to die
But I want to live
I don't want to be in this place
I want to be back home
Because I am too small to die
Why do I need to die?

Adam Zyrek (7)
St Aidan's Catholic Primary Academy, Ilford

Cool Runnings

Me and Nevaeh in Cool Runnings, Jamaica
Feeling over the moon
But petrified we climb to the top
And we get a fright
We go down the slide for the ride of our lives
The water splashing fiercely on both sides
I feel like I'm going fast on a speed boat
Ah the water going down my throat
Blue slide, *splash!*

Janelle Forbes (8)
St Aidan's Catholic Primary Academy, Ilford

Giants

I am in the giant forest.
A giant is stepping on me.
I am so sad.
I am walking and then I see a giant,
Who is about to step on me.
I am with my parents
This is what the giant was doing with me,
Stamping...
Jumping and running...
Stepping...
This is what the giant
Was doing to me!

Bismah Sohail (9)
St Aidan's Catholic Primary Academy, Ilford

My Family As Angels

As I look into the sky
I see my beautiful brother drifting through the sky
Next I see my sister
And then my lovely mother
After that my handsome father
Zooming through the sky

They stop and wait for me
But all I can say to them is,
'Sorry but not tonight
As I am not so bright.'

Thusana Shanthakumar (9)
St Aidan's Catholic Primary Academy, Ilford

The Scariest Time Of My Life!

Once Maida and Dorian had a dinner,
They went to the café called Winner
And ate some Kinders.
They saw a monster, but it was water
And they went in a horse carriage
And then they had a marriage
They went home in a Lamborghini
And had a party with loads of people
And lots of food.

Zoé-Jane O'Leary (8)
St Aidan's Catholic Primary Academy, Ilford

I'm In Diamond Land!

Diamond tree and diamond animals
All I see is light blue
I'm with Matthew standing
On the plains

It was a little hot
So I was going to take
My shoes off but
They were reluctant

Me and Matthew were exhausted
And there was a pond
So we went there to relax.

Shaan Doal (9)
St Aidan's Catholic Primary Academy, Ilford

The Scary Castle

One scary night I saw a kite taking flight and it was
very light
I woke up in the night
And followed the light
With the kite
It took me to a castle and it had a bright light
And the light pointed in a spot
I dug in that spot
And there was a key
The key was gold and quite heavy.

Hannah Maqsud (7)
St Aidan's Catholic Primary Academy, Ilford

Candyland

I see candyfloss clouds
And a gummy bear crowd
With sweet lollipops
And sherbet raindrops
I see Mr and Mrs Cherry Lips
Eating fish and chips
Then go to Princess Poppy's candy house
And she's wearing her pink blouse
I had some Oreo marshmallows
Then I set off home.

Corri Ama Owusu Boateng (8)
St Aidan's Catholic Primary Academy, Ilford

Christmas?

My dad dropped me to school
I ran and saw my friends playing
The playground was full of trees
And flowers and laughing children
The area is so jolly and loud, all in red and white
I felt so happy and excited
Wishing it would never end
And yes. It feels like Christmas to me.

Michael Jacob F Madriaga (6)
St Aidan's Catholic Primary Academy, Ilford

The Yummy Chocolate Factory

C andy everywhere

H ot chocolate river

O h yummy

C hocolate bars

O utside is the giant stash of gigantic,

L ovely candy

A bout the factories chocolate spins

T he chocolate is yummy and beautiful

E veryone was outside.

Remigiusz Skubiszewski (7)
St Aidan's Catholic Primary Academy, Ilford

Living In Yummyland

The gummy grass under my feet
All the yummy things I eat
Chocolate milk drips on my head
Lying in my comfy bed

I'm swinging on strawberry laces
On marshmallows I'm running races
I'm with my parents, my teddy as well
Ringing the pop song sounding bell.

Amara Peters (8)
St Aidan's Catholic Primary Academy, Ilford

Dungeon Of Battle And Horror

W isdom
A nger
R age
S urvival

O ptimus
F urious

S uffering
U nsafe
R egenerated
V ictory
I njury
V ictorious
A tlantic
L aunch.

Micah Thirugnanam Chocken (7)
St Aidan's Catholic Primary Academy, Ilford

Magical Dreams

I'm in a fairy land
There is pink and purple sand
I team up with a fairy
Who loves dairy
I have to kill a bad queen
With my new team
I gain some wings
And some magical things
Now the bad queen is dead
I wish it was real but I'm in my bed!

Tisha Mohammed (10)
St Aidan's Catholic Primary Academy, Ilford

Demon Dolly

Demon Dolly's on
The way to killing me
Right today
I saw the cries
Of terror
As I cried about
My error
Me and Dolly
Strolling by
On the road
In the dark and gloomy night
Never go away
From me and my
Sister Molly again.

Kaci Emmanuel (10)
St Aidan's Catholic Primary Academy, Ilford

The Zombie

I saw Haokan
With a gun
And an evil
Zombie in the farm.
With might
In the night
I had a fright.
After that I
Had to fight.
Fabrice had
My back when
The zombies attack!
When I nearly die
Call Fabrice
He's the guy!

Gabriel Jai Patel (9)
St Aidan's Catholic Primary Academy, Ilford

Candy World

A magical world
Of candy will take you
Off your feet and all
The fairies took me into
This cave full of different fairies
Lots and lots, I felt really scared
Because I did not know
What they were going to do to me
So I ran and I fell into a hole.

Leah McCorkell (9)
St Aidan's Catholic Primary Academy, Ilford

I Dream Of A Dream

I dream of a dream
My whole life in front of me
Gifts of love from above
And me as happy as can be
My future home
My wedding too
All my dreams come true
Children around me
Everyone smiling
I dream of a dream
With wonders ahead of me.

'Derin Adeoye (9)
St Aidan's Catholic Primary Academy, Ilford

Celebrities, Me And Who?

Me and you, you and me
You, me, celebrities and more
You would come and so would I
We would all go on the adventure of our lives

We would go every day for a month
In that month we would have fun with no delays
There is even a lake!

Eden Sofia Zerabruk (8)
St Aidan's Catholic Primary Academy, Ilford

Chibis

As the chibis walked to me
I felt like I was free
Winter, summer, hot or cold
I felt like I was bold

What they said was really nice
Although I slipped on ice
What I did was really good
Although I was not in the mood.

Elton Arulseelan (9)
St Aidan's Catholic Primary Academy, Ilford

Demon Sorrows

Demon, demon why do you follow?
Why do you want my hollow?
Do you want my sorrow?
How shall I react when you kill my sorrow?
Can I act when you turn mellow?
Can I borrow my sorrow
I need my glow but you can keep my hollow.

Hafsah Ali (9)
St Aidan's Catholic Primary Academy, Ilford

The Ice Land

I saw an ice land with mice
Then mice turned into ice
I was shocked
I was spooked
I couldn't even move
Then I saw a girl
The girl was mad
But I didn't care
The girl cared
But she didn't dare.

Faith Tinarwo (9)
St Aidan's Catholic Primary Academy, Ilford

Lost At Sea

I can see water around me and my sister
I can see leaves flying around
I can feel wind blowing on me
Later we went to look for food
And then we found lots and lots of fruit
Later we saw a boat and it saw us and saved us!

Arrabella Nickoll Bekeo-Derby (8)
St Aidan's Catholic Primary Academy, Ilford

Mr Gum And The Kite

Mr Gum was holding a kite and it was a bit of light
Galloping Bill also had a kite
Suddenly the sun turned bright
As galloping Bill galloped in the black, dark night
Mr Gum said, 'What a great night, with some light.'

Naomi Adair (7)
St Aidan's Catholic Primary Academy, Ilford

From The Valley

One restful night
In the valley, searching for food
I can't see in the dark
I am scared, what should I do?
I will not die from my heart
I will survive in the night
I will make a shelter
I will be alright.

Rytis Januska (7)
St Aidan's Catholic Primary Academy, Ilford

Gareth Bale

My name is Gareth Bale
I'm from Wales

I like the waves at sea
I like drinking tea

I don't like coffee
I just love toffee

I like playing ball
I'm not that tall.

Ashllyn Amirthanayagam (9)
St Aidan's Catholic Primary Academy, Ilford

Whatever I Want

I can see my fingers clicking every day
It makes me happy, in each and every way
I worked for some farmers, and patted the hay
I work with the farmers, to buy some games
Then I can click on my console each and every day

Darrius Griffith (8)
St Aidan's Catholic Primary Academy, Ilford

Race The Jet

One day me and Charlie went to a place
Called Race Ride
There were famous, fantastic rides
The race was going to start
It was about to crash
Oh no! I was so close to crashing
Oh so close!
Yes I won.

Darren Ramesh (8)
St Aidan's Catholic Primary Academy, Ilford

Electronic Land

Electronic Land is a magical place
Where you can make your own video games
Make a robot of your dreams
Or make electronic ice cream
Nice and cool, now make your game
Every machine can make games quickly.

Rahul Gupta (8)
St Aidan's Catholic Primary Academy, Ilford

Dreamworld

Last night I had a weird dream
It started with a clap
And ended with a scream

The sky was black with a crack
The clouds were as blue as a screw
With a magical keyboard for you.

Pranav Raju (8)
St Aidan's Catholic Primary Academy, Ilford

Tropical Jungle With A Kite

Me and my best friends were with a kite
And suddenly the sun turned bright
I saw a kite and the kite had a light
And the light was a bit bright
And I saw a kite
On a windy night.

Vanessa Adomako (7)
St Aidan's Catholic Primary Academy, Ilford

The Half-Broken Kite

One night I saw a kite
It had a knight and the colour was red
The girl flying it was called Ned
I also saw a chocolate house
It was gigantic
It was delicious outside and inside.

Lauryn Anaekwe (8)
St Aidan's Catholic Primary Academy, Ilford

Candy Hotel

I had a dream of a chocolate river and lollipops
And marshmallow houses and chocolate syrup
I was riding a candy unicorn with an orange gummy
bear
We were in the hotel of sour unicorn.

Priya Panesar (8)
St Aidan's Catholic Primary Academy, Ilford

I Wish To Be A Dandelion

Dandelions are lovely and look like a beautiful flower
Dandelions smell nice and lovely
Dandelions are white like a bird
Dandelions are sweet and true
Dandelions are wonderful.

Rachel Colette Fernando (6)
St Aidan's Catholic Primary Academy, Ilford

Zombies

It was night
I was in a fight
But I got a fright
Because I was in fright night
The costume was really tight
So I might not win the fight
Because it's not bright.

Hassan Ali (9)
St Aidan's Catholic Primary Academy, Ilford

Guy Fawkes And Me

The fifth of November is a special day
Because it is not far from my birthday
Bangs and crashes are what fireworks make
Sometimes they are scary but often great.

Khyra Maynard (6)
St Aidan's Catholic Primary Academy, Ilford

My Unicorn

Anyone seen my unicorn?
She is magical and she has a horn
Anyone seen my unicorn?
She's pretty and pink
Anyone seen my unicorn?

Esther Mulungi (6)
St Aidan's Catholic Primary Academy, Ilford

Flowers

Short and beautiful
White and colourful
Bright and plentiful.

Hannah Thammadi (6)
St Aidan's Catholic Primary Academy, Ilford

YoungWriters
Est.1991

YOUNG WRITERS INFORMATION

We hope you have enjoyed reading this book – and
that you will continue to in the coming years.

If you're a young writer who enjoys reading and creative writing,
or the parent of an enthusiastic poet or story writer,
do visit our website **www.youngwriters.co.uk**. Here you will
find free competitions, workshops and games, as well as
recommended reads, a poetry glossary and our blog.

If you would like to order further copies of this book,
or any of our other titles, then please give us a
call or visit **www.youngwriters.co.uk**.

Young Writers
Remus House
Coltsfoot Drive
Peterborough
PE2 9BF
(01733) 890066
info@youngwriters.co.uk